YOUNG EUROPEAN ARCHITECTS

daab

INTRODUCTION

European architecture is distinguished by a variety of forms and styles. This building diversity is influenced by architects and agencies throughout all of Europe. Many "heads" of various nationalities with a diversity of approaches and concepts contribute to this multiplicity with their creative ideas and unconventional solutions.

There are several young architects in the bunch. New offices, recent graduates, young-at-heart, interdisciplinary career changers and lone warriors provide insight into their work with both the realized projects and visions for the future depicted in this book. Today, architects work less and less within geographical borders. Nowadays, they think more globally, since competitions are increasingly advertised on an international basis. These competitions provide new architects and relatively young and inexperienced agencies with the chance of vying for larger jobs along with the well-known and well-established stars of the branch. Many of the featured buildings illustrate this continual development of borderless building. It is no longer clearly visible in whose heads they were conceived and where they were built. Europe is not only getting smaller in a political sense; this fusion is also evident in architecture. That is precisely why it is so exciting to witness how consciously the architects play with the clichés of their countries and actual realities. They work with various styles, experiment, reinterpret and inspire contemplation, often with a slightly ironic touch. Following years of a trend toward great austerity and reduction, new agencies are now reaching for unconventional forms and colors with courage and wit, revealing new images of architecture. Conspicuous features include more ornamentation, sophisticated surface structures, floral patterns, previously unconventional material combinations and loud, bright colors. Anything goes that captures attention.

Young European Architects provides insight and an overview of the architectural scene in Europe, and with the aid of portraits and short explanatory texts, presents the featured agencies and architects and their websites.

Europäische Architektur zeichnet sich durch eine Vielfalt an Formen und Stilen aus. Diese Mannigfaltigkeit an Bauten ist geprägt von Architekten und Büros aus ganz Europa. Viele „Köpfe" unterschiedlicher Herkunft tragen mit verschiedenen Denkansätzen und Konzepten, mit neuen, kreativen Ideen und unkonventionellen Lösungsansätzen zu dieser Abwechslung bei.

Viele Junge sind dabei. Neue Büros, Studienabgänger, jung gebliebene, interdisziplinäre Quereinsteiger und Einzelkämpfer, die in diesem Buch mit bereits realisierten Projekten, aber auch Zukunftsvisionen Einblicke in ihre Arbeit geben. Der Architekt arbeitet heute immer weniger in geographischen Grenzen. Architekten denken heutzutage noch globaler, da Wettbewerbe vermehrt international ausgeschrieben sind. Sie geben Berufsanfängern und relativ jungen, unerfahrenen Architekturbüros die potenzielle Chance neben namhaften und renommierten Stars der Branche auch an größere Aufträge zu kommen. Viele vorgestellte Gebäude veranschaulichen diese stetige Entwicklung der grenzenlosen Bautätigkeit. Sie lassen nicht mehr auf Anhieb erkennen, in welchen Köpfen sie entstanden und wo sie gebaut worden sind. Europa rückt nicht nur im politischen Sinne zusammen, auch in der Architektur ist diese Fusion zu beobachten. Gerade deswegen ist es spannend zu sehen, wie bewusst Architekten mit dem Klischee eines Landes und seiner tatsächlichen Realität spielen. Sie arbeiten mit verschiedenen Stilmitteln, experimentieren, interpretieren neu und regen zum Nachdenken an, gern mit leicht ironischem Unterton. Nach einem jahrelangen Trend zu großer Schlichtheit und Reduktion greifen junge Büros mit Mut und Witz zu unkonventionellen Formen und Farben und bringen neue Erscheinungsbilder der Architektur hervor. So fallen wieder vermehrt Ornamente, differenzierte Oberflächenstrukturen, florale Muster, bisher unübliche Materialkombinationen und laute, knallige Farben ins Auge. Erlaubt ist, was gefällt und Aufmerksamkeit erregt.

Young European Architects gibt einen Ein- und Überblick in die Architekturszene Europas und stellt mit Hilfe von Portraits, kurzen, erläuternden Texten die vertretenen Büros und Architekten mit ihren Webseiten vor.

L'architecture européenne se distingue par une variété de formes et de styles. Cette diversité des édifices résulte des apports d'architectes et de bureaux d'étude de toute l'Europe. De nombreuses "têtes" d'origine diverse contribuent à cette diversité avec des pensées et des concepts différents, des idées neuves, créatives et des solutions non conventionnelles. Beaucoup d'entre eux sont jeunes. De nouveaux bureaux d'étude, des jeunes diplômés, des personnes jeunes d'esprit, des professionnels issus d'autres disciplines et des combattants solitaires qui présentent dans cet ouvrage leur travail non seulement par le biais de projets déjà terminés, mais aussi de leurs visions du futur.

A notre époque, les architectes sont de moins en moins confinés à des frontières géographiques. Ils ont aujourd'hui une vision plus mondiale, les concours étant de plus en plus souvent adjugés par voie de soumission au niveau international. De cette manière, les débutants ainsi que les bureaux d'étude relativement jeunes et inexpérimentés peuvent éventuellement obtenir également de gros contrats à côté de stars réputées et renommées de cette branche. De nombreux édifices ici présentés illustrent cette évolution constante de l'architecture sans frontière. Il est désormais impossible de deviner d'emblée l'origine de leurs concepteurs et le lieu où ils ont été construits. L'Europe s'amalgame non seulement au sens politique, mais on observe également cette fusion dans l'architecture. C'est justement pour cette raison qu'il est intéressant de voir avec quelle sûreté les architectes jouent avec les clichés d'un pays et ses réalités. Ils travaillent avec divers styles, ils expérimentent, réinterprètent et invitent à réfléchir, souvent avec une touche d'ironie. Après une tendance à la grande simplicité et au réductionnisme qui a duré des années, les jeunes bureaux d'étude n'hésitent pas à recourir, avec courage et humour, à des formes et des couleurs non conventionnelles, générant ainsi de nouvelles manifestations de l'architecture. Nous voyons ainsi réapparaître des ornements, des structures superficielles différenciées, des motifs floraux, des combinaisons de matériaux jusqu'ici inhabituelles ainsi que des couleurs vives et criardes. Tout est permis, pourvu que cela plaise et attire l'attention.

Young European Architects donne à ses lecteurs un panorama de la situation actuelle dans l'architecture européenne et présente les bureaux d'étude et les architectes qui y figurent, et leurs sites web, au moyen de portraits et de courts textes explicatifs.

La arquitectura europea se caracteriza por una variedad de formas y estilos que resulta de los aportes de arquitectos y estudios de arquitectura de toda Europa. Muchas "cabezas" de diferente origen aportan enfoques y conceptos, con ideas nuevas y creativas y soluciones no convencionales, a esa diversidad. Muchos son jóvenes. Estudios nuevos, jóvenes recién recibidos, jóvenes de espíritu, profesionales de otras disciplinas que se pasan a la arquitectura y luchadores solitarios que presentan en este libro su trabajo no solamente por medio de proyectos ya terminados, sino también con sus proyectos futuros.

En la actualidad, los arquitectos trabajan cada vez menos dentro de límites geográficos. Tienen que tener un pensamiento global, dado que la mayoría de las licitaciones son internacionales. Así es como principiantes y estudios de arquitectura relativamente nuevos y con poca experiencia acceden a la oportunidad de conseguir proyectos más grandes junto a los profesionales reconocidos y famosos del sector. Muchos de los edificios presentados reflejan este permanente desarrollo de la construcción sin límites. Ya no es posible saber a simple vista de dónde son las personas que los concibieron o dónde fueron construidos. Europa no solamente se está amalgamando políticamente, sino que la fusión se observa también en la arquitectura. Justamente por ello resulta interesante ver con qué seguridad juegan los arquitectos con los clichés de un país y sus realidades. Trabajan con diferentes estilos, experimentan, reinterpretan y llaman a la reflexión, muchas veces con un matiz de ironía. Después de una tendencia que duró varios años hacia la simpleza y el reduccionismo, los estudios nuevos recurren con valentía y humor a las formas y colores no convencionales, y generan nuevas manifestaciones de la arquitectura. Así es como vemos nuevamente más ornamentación, estructuras superficiales diferenciadas, motivos florales, combinaciones de materiales inusuales, y colores fuertes y llamativos. Se permite todo lo que gusta y llama la atención.

Young European Architects brinda un panorama de la situación actual de la arquitectura europea, presentando arquitectos y estudios de arquitectura (y sus páginas web) por medio de textos breves.

L'architettura europea si distingue per la sua ricchezza di forme e stili. Questa varietà di costruzioni nasce dal fatto che gli architetti e i loro studi provengano da tutti i paesi dell'Europa. Molte „teste" d'origini diverse contribuiscono a questa molteplicità con differenti modi di pensare e concepire, con le loro nuove e creative idee e con soluzioni inconsuete. Molti tra loro sono giovani, c'è anche chi ha lasciato gli studi o chi con la mentalità del giovane entra da un altro settore, ci sono nuovi studi d'architetto e combattenti individuali. Tutti coloro presentano in questo volume le proprie opere e visioni del futuro.

L'architetto contemporaneo lavora sempre meno all'interno di limiti geografici. Gli architetti d'oggi pensano più globalmente, visto che sempre più appalti sono banditi a livello internazionale, dando ai novellini del mestiere ed a studi d'architetto giovani e con poca esperienza la possibilità di partecipare a commesse anche importanti, accanto ai rinomati e famosi leader del settore. Molti tra gli edifici presentati illustrano questo continuo sviluppo dell'attività edile senza frontiere. Non è più possibile riconoscere a prima vista quale testa li abbia escogitati e dove siano stati costruiti. L'Europa s'accosta non soltanto politicamente, ma tale fusione si evidenzia anche nell'architettura. È proprio per questo motivo che diventa affascinante osservare come gli architetti consapevolmente giochino con il clichè di un paese e con la sua effettiva realtà. Lavorano con diversi mezzi stilistici, sperimentano, riinterpretano e invitano alla riflessione, spesso con una sottile ironia. Dopo un lungo trend verso la semplicità e la riduzione, oggi gli studi giovani con coraggio e spirito scelgono forme e colori non convenzionali e creano così nuovi aspetti dell'architettura. Ritornano in vista più ornamenti, svariate strutture di superfici, ornamenti floreali, inconsuete combinazioni di materiali e colori forti e accesi. È permesso ciò che piace e che richiama l'attenzione.

Per mezzo di ritratti e brevi spiegazioni, Young European Architects presenta in dettaglio ed in generale la scena dell'architettura in Europa con i suoi studi d'architetto e gli architetti, con le loro pagine web.

3LHD | ZAGREB, CROATIA

Saša Begović, Marko Dabrović, Tanja Grozdanić, Silvije Novak

3LHD was created in Zagreb, Croatia in 1994 by four founding partners. Today, the collaborative office employs eighteen architects interested in the integration of architecture, art, and (urban) landscape. Their work has been awarded with numerous local and international awards, and their members frequently reach out to young designers as teachers, lecturers, and critics.

www.3lhd.com

1 Croatian Pavilion on EXPO 2005, *Aichi, Japan*
2 Memorial Bridge 2000, *Rijeka*

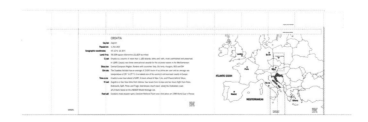

Kap vode, zrno soli.
A drop of water, a grain of salt.
一滴の水, 一粒の塩

1

1

2

2

3RW ARCHITECTS | BERGEN, NORWAY

Sixten Rahlff, Espen Rahlff, Haakon R. Rasmussen,
Jakob Røsvik, Eirik W. Astrup, Susanne Puchberger,
Henning Frønsda

The Bergen-based 3RW Architects was established in 1999.
The eight-person design team works within an extended
architectonic sphere and at a number of different scales;
their portfolio contains projects ranging from industrial design to urban planning.

www.3rw.no

1 National tourist road, *Geiranger Trollstigen*
2 Addition to 17th-century farm, *Habakka*

2

4DS | PRAGUE, CZECH REPUBLIC
Milan Hakl, Lubos Zemen, Pavel Mikulenka, Jan Drahozal,
Radek Janosik, Eva Zemenova, Silvia Grebáčová

Founded in 1998 in Prague with a second office in South Bohemia that opened in 2003, the 4DS team currently employs six architects. 4DS explores the formal properties of a variety of aspects in the built environment, from zone planning and civil architecture to housing and interior design. Their success is underscored by two awards and several features in books and magazines.

www.4ds.cz

1 Family house, *Vcelna*
2 Interior house, *Kozinec*

1

2

51N4E | BRUSSELS, BELGIUM

Johan Anrys, Freek Persyn, Peter Swinnen

51N4E is a Brussels-based office that concerns itself with architecture, urban design, and other (currently unpredictable) space-related issues. The three partners, working in a 12 members-team, revel in the possibilities of these "space productions" for reconfiguring existing urban conditions. Only three years after establishing their practice in 2000, 51N4E won the Maaskant Prize for Young Architects.

www.51n4e.com

1 Lamot – cultural convention center 2005, *Mechelen, Belgium*
2 Groeningemuseum 2003, *Bruges, Belgium*

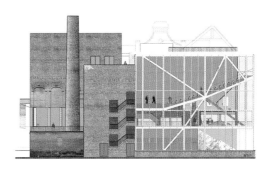

6A ARCHITECTS | HOLBORN, UK
Tom Emerson, Stephanie Macdonald

6a Architects was founded by Tom Emerson and Stephanie Macdonald after they met as students at the Royal College of Art. They produce work on multiple scales, from product and exhibition design to art galleries and large-scale housing developments. Their work dissolves the boundaries between the familiar and the unknown and the practice has gained critical success for its simplicity and material invention.

www.6a.co.uk

1 Hairywood, *temporary public space, London, in cooperation with Eley Kishimoto*
2 Oki-ni flagshipstore 2002

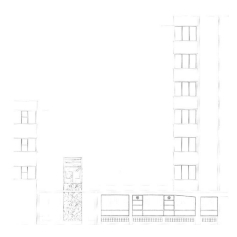

2

A69 – ARCHITEKTI | PRAGUE, CZECH REPUBLIC

Boris Redčenkov , Prokop Tomášek, Jaroslav Wertig

In the relatively short period of its existence (the atelier was established in 1994), A69 – architekti has earned the attention of the design media with the quality and consistency of their built and speculative work. The Dr. Peták Sanatorium was a finalist for the Grand Prix 2001, and was nominated for the European Union's 2003 Mies van der Rohe Award for contemporary architecture.

www.a69.cz

1 Villa Park Strahov 2003, *Prague*
2 Dr. Peták Sanatorium 2001,
   Construction of balneotherapeutic sanatorium,
   Františkovy Lázně, Czech Republic

AART | ÅRHUS C, DENMARK
Anders Strange, Anders Tyrrestrup,
Torben Skovbjerg Larsen

AART, founded in 2000. is a high-performance team of young designers and technicians that deliver full-service advising in the field of architecture. They challenge and rethink the Nordic architectural tradition with a direct focus on social responsibility, resources, economy, and time. Many of their projects are result of winning design competitions.

www.aart.dk

1 Sletten outdoor scout Center
2 Bikuben student hostel

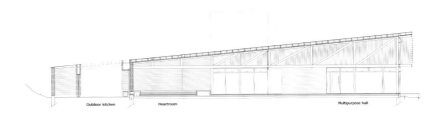

Outdoor kitchen   Heartroom   Multipurpose hall

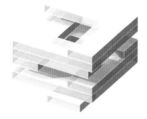

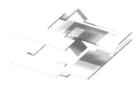

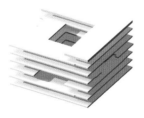

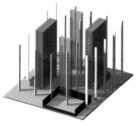

2

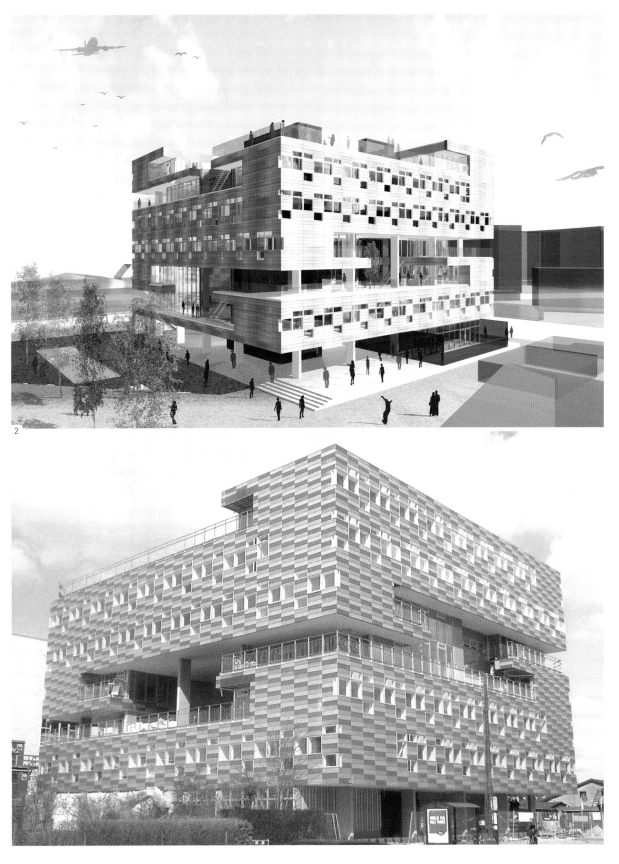

2

AFF | BERLIN, GERMANY

Martin Fröhlich, Sven Fröhlich, Torsten Lockl

The team of AFF, together since 1999, works through a collaborative, democratic process of flexible relationships and exchanges of information. Many of their projects, such as a nursing home, an archive, and a cafeteria for the university in Berlin, are competition entries intended for sites in the former East Germany.

www.aff-architekten.com

1 House Seeger, *Weimar*
2 Sächsisches Bergarchiv
3 Formsteinwand Haus Zivcec
4 Sanitäranlage IJBZ Barleber See, *Magdeburg*

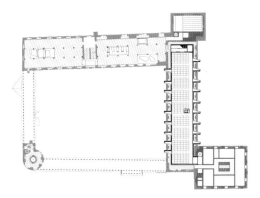

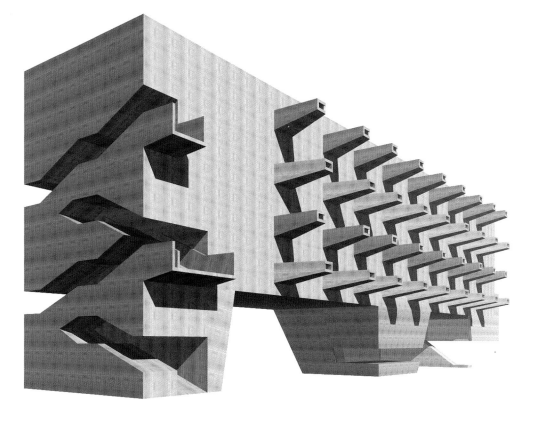

2

3

4

AKSL ARHITEKTI | LJUBLJANA, SLOVENIA
Spela Leskovic and Ales Kosak

AKSL arhitekti was founded in December 2000 by Spela Leskovic and Ales Kosak. Since then they have taken on two more staff members and have been involved into over forty different projects. They are an interdisciplinary office concentrating not only on architecture but also on interior design and scenography.

www.aksl.org

1 Renovation of single-family house 2004
2 Shop "Sailing point" 2003

2

ALA | HELSINKI, FINLAND

Juho Grönholm, Antti Nousjoki, Janne Teräsvirta,
Samuli Woolston

ALA Architects Ltd is a Helsinki-based architecture firm founded by four partners in 2004. Today ALA has a permanent staff of twelve and an additional office in Norway. ALA develops and implements practical, construction-friendly architecture based on an understanding of design and construction methodology. Their work responds to the specific needs of the client as well as the surrounding environment.

www.ala-a.com

1 Performing arts center for Sørlandet 2010, *Kristiansand*
2 Urban chapel "Sasso", *competition 2004, Helsinki*
3 Campus de la Justicia, *competition 2005, Madrid*

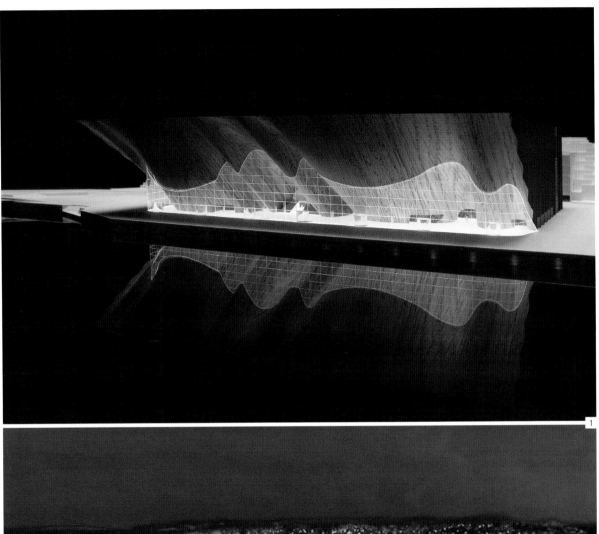

2

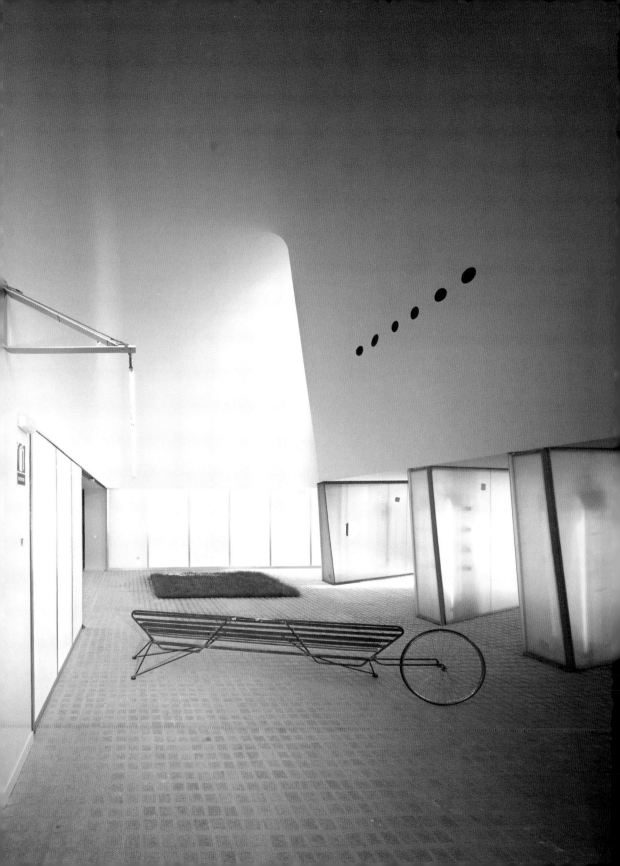

ANDRÉS JAQUE | MADRID, SPAIN

Since his office opened in 2000, Andrés Jacque has won a number of competitions, published in international magazines, and exhibited in Hellerau (Dresden), Lima, and Madrid. Andrés Jaque's theoretical and critical work focuses on innovative architecture that challenges existing political structures.

www.andresjaque.net

Casa Sacerdotal Diocesana de Plasencia 2004

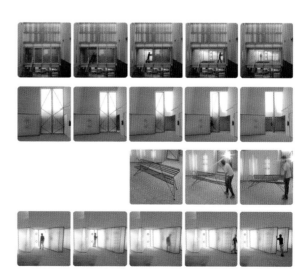

ARCHIPOLIS | VILNIUS, LITHUNIA

Tomas Masiulis, Virginijus Gerdvilis, Mantas Volbekas

Archopolis was established in 1995 with the objective of realizing high-quality architecture. The studio has a diverse practice, including housing projects, office buildings, and industrial facilities-both ground-up projects and renovations. The design team takes responsibility for all aspects of the design process down to the building permits and working drawings, and collaborates with professional partners in all specialized areas.

www.architektai.org

1 Interior of VZDRMC 2004, *environment for students in Vilnius*
2 Printing house 2005, *Vilnius*

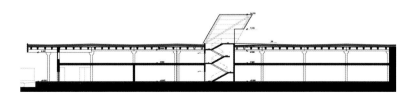

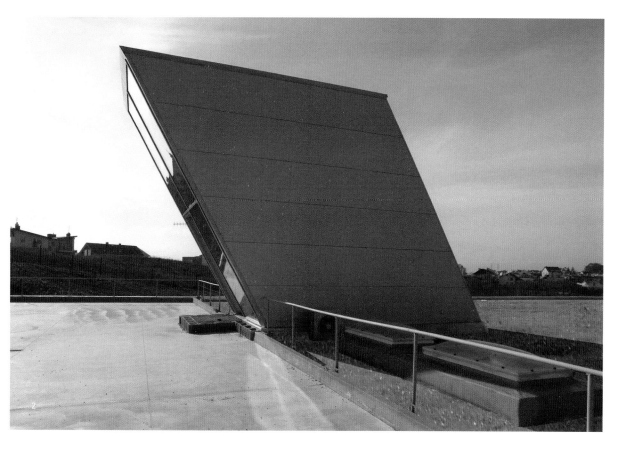

ARCHITECTSLAB | **BRUSSELS, HASSELT, BELGIUM**
William Froidmont, Peter-Paul Piot, Bart America

Architectslab was founded in 2002 as a design collective for architecture, interior design, and urbanism. All three principals studied architecture and interior design at colleges in Brussels and Hasselt and worked in several different design studios before they combined forces in their own studio. Architectslab tries to produce designs in a timeless and functional – yet personal – architectural language.

www.architectslab.com

1 Restaurant 1220
2 Offices L

1

2

ATX ARCHITEKTI | BRNO, CZECH REPUBLIC

Tomáš Beránek, Zdenek Eichler, Rostislav Jakubec

ATX ARCHITEKTI was founded in 1998 by Tomáš Beránek, Zdenek Eichler, and Rostislav Jakubec. The main objective of their projects is a quest for an individual approach to spatial problems through the development of architectonic form. The resulting buildings, whether large public institutions or small residences, have a singular aesthetic that cannot be replicated.

www.atxarchitekti.cz

1 The cultural centrum Brno, *competition*
2 House on the square Boskovice
3 House Blansko

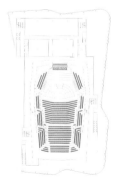
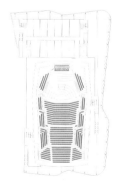

BKARK | TRONDHEIM, NORWAY
Geir Brendeland, Olav Kristoffersen

BKARK began in 2002 when Geir Brendeland and Olav Krist-offersen left their jobs in Oslo to get a firsthand feeling for the context of an apartment building project in Trondheim in mid-north Norway. In their search for the true spirit of the place – a combination of the natural environment, history, and people – the architects found a design strategy that incorporates modern and traditional approaches to building.

www.bkark.no

1 Svartlamoen, Trondheim 2005, *dwelling for city's alternative population*
2 Berlinbox 2005, *part of the Svartlamoen housing*

2

2

BOTTEGA+EHRHARDT | STUTTGART, GERMANY
Giorgio Bottega, Henning Ehrhardt

Before starting their own office in 1998, Giorgio Bottega and Henning Ehrhardt worked for several different architecture offices in Locarno, Barcelona, Munich, Zurich, and New York. Nowadays most of their projects are located in and around Stuttgart, but they have been published in magazines in Germany and abroad.

www.be-arch.com

1 Haus M 2004, *Stuttgart*
2 Haus U 2002, *Ludwigsburg*
3 Haus S 2002, *Ludwigsburg*
4 Zollinger Halle 2002, *Werbeagentur H2e, Ludwigsburg*

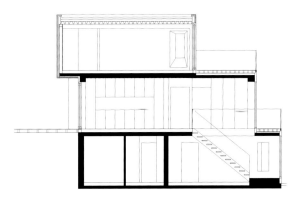

2

3

4

BOUQUELLE_POPOFF | BRUSSELS, BELGIUM
Nicolas Bouquelle, Johannie Popoff

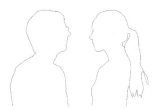

Johannie Popoff and Nicolas Bouquelle met in 1991 during their architecture studies at the ISACF-La Cambre in Brussels. They started working together as "bouquelle_popoff architectes" in 2002 for the Domestic Warehouse project, which gained critical acclaim for its innovative concept as an alternative living space.

www.bouquellepopoff-architectes.be

1 Veranda on Piles 2005, *extension of a house, Brussels*
2 Domestic Warehouse 2002, *loft, Brussels*

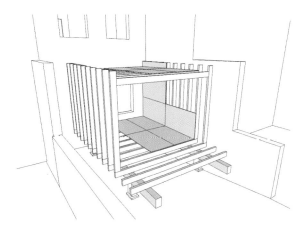

2

BRISAC GONZALEZ | LONDON, UK
Cécile Brisac, Edgar Gonzalez

In a relatively short period of time Brisac Gonzalez, established in 1999, has accrued a diverse body of work that includes museums, town halls, concert halls, and mixed-used facilities. Their early success was ensured later that year when the practice won an international two-stage competition for the Museum of World Culture in Gothenburg, Sweden. The 11,000-square-meter museum opened in December 2004 and was awarded the Kasper Salins Prize for best building in Sweden.

www.brisacgonzalez.com

Museum of world culture 2004, *interior fitout, Gothenburg, Sweden*

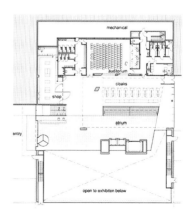

BWM ARCHITECTS | VIENNA, AUSTRIA
Erich Bernard, Daniela Walten, Johann Moser

BWM Architects and Partners is a studio for architecture, planning, and design based in Vienna since 2004. Their recent work includes the Manner Confectionery, the John Harris Medical Spa, and the new Stiefelkönig Shoe Boutique in Vienna, as well as the Museum of Regional Ethnology in Graz and Wien Museum in Vienna.

www.bwm.at

1 John Harris 2005, *alteration of a salesroom into an exclusive medical spa, Vienna*
2 Folk Museum 2003, *reconstruction, redesign of the existing museum and the permanent exhibition hall, Graz*

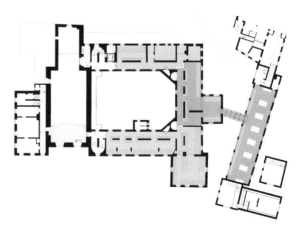

CASANOVA + HERNÁNDEZ | ROTTERDAM, THE NETHERLANDS
Helena Casanova, Jesús Hernández

In 2001 Casanova + Hernandez Architecten was established in Rotterdam in order to experiment with and build a sustainable urban habitat for the 21st-century. To this end, they combine aspects of urban planning, landscape architecture, and architecture in their practice. This global understanding of design is explored in every project, from the largest planning scale to the smallest technical details.

www.casanova-hernandez.com

1 Tittot Art Glass Museum 2004, *Taipei, Taiwan*
2 Patio-Villas 2005, *Patio-dwelling, Groningen*

COMPLIZEN | HALLE/SAALE, BERLIN, GERMANY

Andreas Haase, Tore Dobberstein

complizen is a young office for architecture, communication, and urban development in Halle/Saale and Berlin, Germany. As a part of the first generation of architects dealing with the transformation of post-socialist East Germany into an open society with leisure- and event-oriented architecture, complizen employs traditional crafts and skills in new and unknown ways.

www.complizen.de

Kappa marketing agency 2003

DCM-STUDIO | BRATISLAVA, SLOVAKIA
Dana Čupková-Myers in collaboration with Martin Myers

DCm-STUDIO is a practice engaged in both real and speculative projects. It explores new spatial organizations through the systematic subversion of cliché driven architectural models. Dana, the principal of DCm-STUDIO, collaborates with Martin on a project to project basis. As an architect/artist collaborative they employ a conceptual strategy to maneuver within the boundaries of art and architecture to investigate new areas of overlap within these disciplines.

www.dcm-studio.net

1 Roof space renovation
2 Art-Work–Art-Museum, *installation in Kunsthaus Wien*
3 D+S House, *weekend house for flood plane*

BEGINNING OF EARLY BRONZE AGE IN CHINA ■

RISE OF BUDDHISM IN INDIA ■

CAROLINGIAN ■

FOUNDATION OF HOLY ROMAN EMPIRE ■

ROMANESQUE (NORMAN) ■

BATTLE OF HASTINGS ■

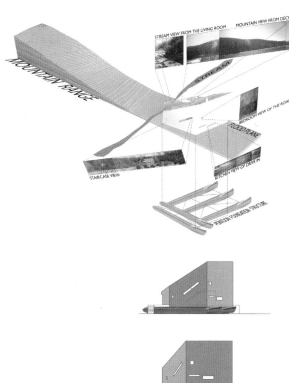

DEKLEVA GREGORIČ ARHITEKTI | LJUBLJANA, SLOVENIA
Aljoša Dekleva, Tina Gregorič

The work of Dekleva Gregorič spans a variety of architectural projects with a conceptual, intense approach to structuring space. By challenging the use of materials and exposing their true natures, the firm's buildings have an industrial, hard-edged feel without losing touch with the human-scale experience.

www.dekleva-gregoric.com

1 XXS House 2004, *Ljubljana, Slovenia, urban holiday home*
2 Housing L 2005, *Sezana, Slovenia, collective housing, with Tina Rugelj, Flavio Coddou, Lea Kovic*

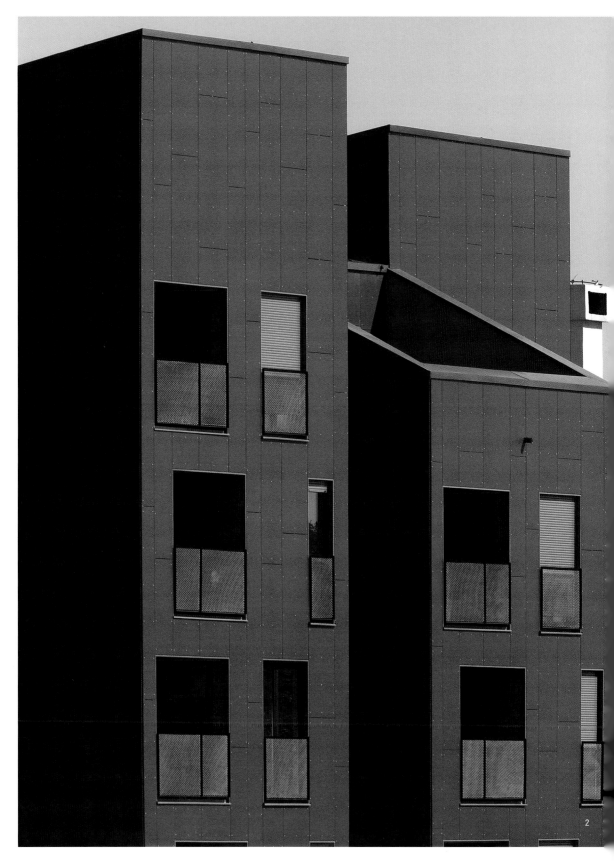

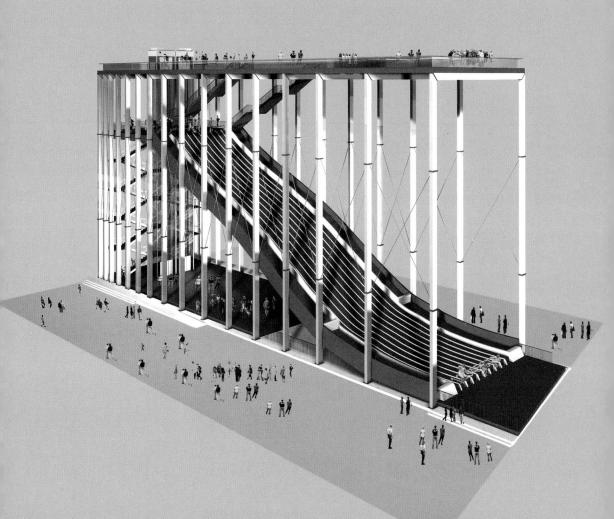

ENCORE HEUREUX | PARIS, FRANCE
Nicola Delon, Julien Choppin

Encore heureux was founded in 2001 in Paris by Nicola De-lon and Julien Choppin – two freshly graduated architecture students. In realized projects as well as conceptual de-signs, their work is visionary, ephemeral, and imaginative. Their studio also produces stunning architectural render-ings and graphics.

www.encoreheureux.org

1 Tobboggan Olympique 2004, *competition with JES Design*
2 Wagons scenes 2005, *with P.E. Schirr-Bonnans*

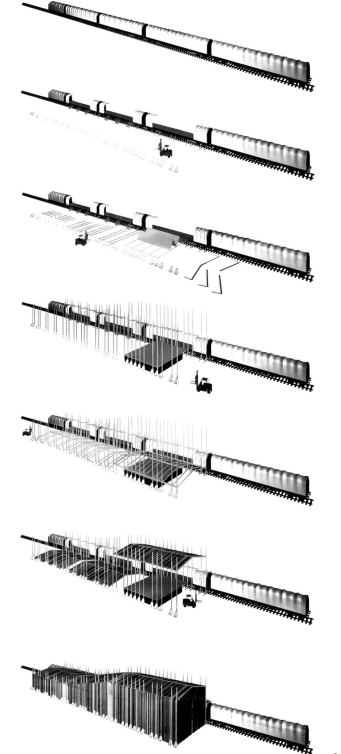

2

ENOTA | LJUBLJANA, SLOVENIA

Milan Tomac, Dean Lah

Enota was founded in 1998 with the ambition to create a contemporary and critical architectural practice of an open type. Currently there are nine active members in the office. In past years Enota won several architectural competitions, gave lectures on their design philosophies, and published their work in various media.

www.enota.si

1 nkbm, *working space*
2 Hotel Sotelia
3 Termalija

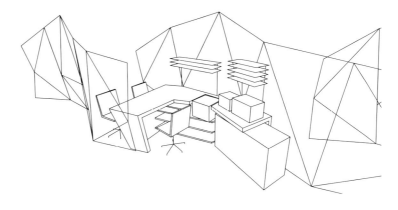

FKL | DUBLIN, IRELAND

Michelle Fagan, Paul Kelly, Gary Lysaght

FKL Architects was formed in 1998 by Dublin School of Architecture graduates Michelle Fagan, Paul Kelly, and Gary Lysaght. Committed to pragmatic and contemporary design, FKL Architects focuses on the real-world application of abstract ideas to built form. Each project that comes into their office begins from scratch, becoming a specific solution to that client's needs, the programmatic conditions, and site context.

www.fklarchitects.com

1 Brick House Milltown Path
2 Baldoyle Library and Local Area Offices
3 Silicon Software Systems

1

3

FÜNDC | ROTTERDAM, THE NETHERLANDS
César García Guerra, Paz Martin

FünDC's objective is to become a unified source of multidisciplinary design solutions. To this end, fünDC offers in-house expertise in the fields of architecture, interior and furniture design, graphic and image design, branding, and urban design. For those fields outside of fünDC's main focus, the team reaches out to a network of their colleagues to provide a holistic design concept.

www.fundc.com

NCC, New Cultural Center 2007

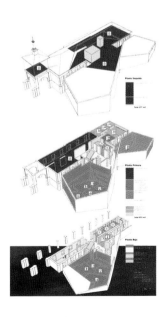

FUHRIMANN HÄCHLER I ZURICH, SWITZERLAND

Gabrielle Hächler, Andreas Fuhrimann

Gabrielle Hächler, who spent part of her art history and architecture studies in India, and Andreas Fuhrimann, who also worked as a lecturer in interior design at the School of Design and Crafts, started Fuhrimann Hächler in 1995. From a small hut in the Alps to a hotel bar, from artists' housing to public infrastructure, their work successfully adapts to diverse sites and situations.

www.afgh.ch

1 Appartmenthouse in Zürich 2004
2 Pavilion at the lake of Zürich 2004
3 Holydayhouse on the Rigi 2005, *in the Alpes of Switzerland*

1

3

GÜLLER GÜLLER | ROTTERDAM, THE NETHERLANDS | ZURICH, SWITZERLAND

Mathis Güller, Michael Güller

Güller Güller, based in Rotterdam and Zurich, approaches the changing conditions in urban design from an unexpected and integral point of view. Through their diverse projects, they suggest a fresh and comprehensive planning and design culture that combines the requirements and possibilities of architecture, urban design, and infrastructural planning. Realization of 'La Fleur du Flon' stopped due to financial cut-backs of festival sponsors.

www.ggau.net

'La Fleur du Flon', First prize award, *former industrial area "Flon" in Lausanne*

HAKES ASSOCIATES | LONDON, UK
Julian Hakes, Cari-Jane Hakes

The award-winning designs of this husband-and-wife team demonstrate their interest in the representation of architectural space through drawing, painting, and 3D computer montage. Julian and Cari-Jane's work is heavily influenced by their research pursuits, including the spatiality of the body through choreographed movement and the role of the perception of light and acoustics in space.

www.hakes.co.uk

1 Wycoller visitors center 2002, *spaces and possibilities for exhibition, dance, theatre and art installations*
2 The Mobius Bridge 2005, *Finzels Reach, Bristol*

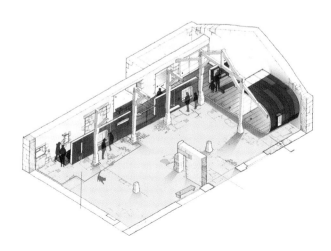

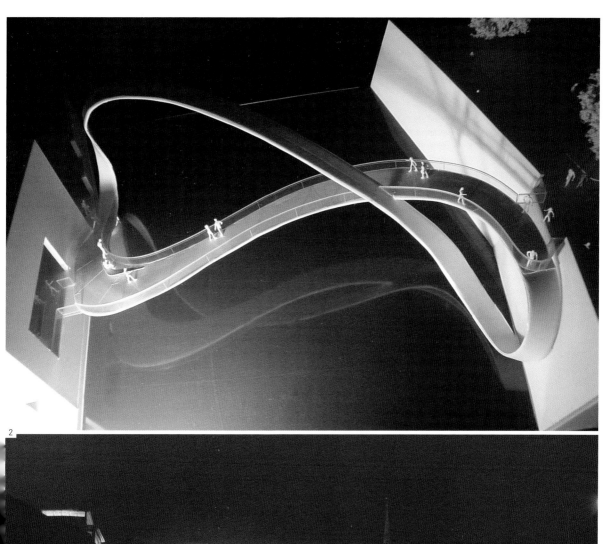

HALMI POLAKOVIČ | BRATISLAVA, SLOVAKIA
Roman Halmi, Stefan Polakovič

Roman Halmi and Stefan Polakoviič both graduated from the university in Bratislava and gathered knowledge at diverse Slovakian architecture offices before starting FHP architekti in 1998. The office, which changed into Halmi Polakovič architects in 2004, captures the dynamism of human activity in their residential and commercial designs.

www.hpa.sk

1 Ungerloft
2 Villa V
3 Dunajska
4 Weekendhouse 1999, *Potôň*

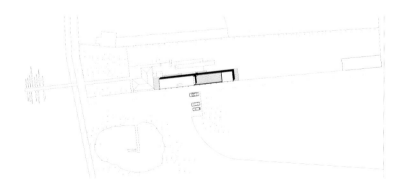

HERI&SALLI | VIENNA, AUSTRIA
Heribert Wolfmayr, Josef Saller

Heri&Salli is Heribert Wolfmayr and Josef Saller, who both received their diplomas in architecture in Graz, Austria in 1999. Before starting their own business in 2004, they collected experience and know-how at other renowned architecture offices. Their work clarifies and enriches a conceptual starting point through formal and visual connections.

www.heriundsalli.com

1 Austriaarchitektur 2005, *exhibition scheme,*
  Galerie Aedes / East in Berlin
2 Schleierraum 2004, *Künstlerhaus Wien, Austria*

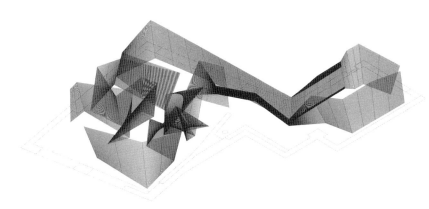

2

MANUEL HERZ | COLOGNE, GERMANY
Manuel Herz

Manuel Herz studied architecture at the Architectural Association in London and has taught at the Bartlett School of Architecture and the Berlage Institute. He set up his own office in Cologne in 2000. In addition to his investigative design work, Herz also researches and writes on issues of architecture and migration.

www.manuelherz.com

1 "Legal/Illegal" 2003, *a mixed-use building in an infill site in Cologne*
2 Ceramic Facade of the Jewish Community Center 2004, *Mainz*
3 Ashdod Museum of Art 2003, *with Eyal Weizman, Rafi Segal*

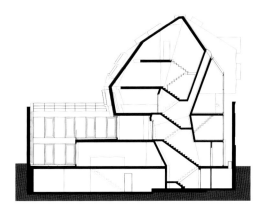

1

2

HILD UND K | MUNICH, GERMANY
Andreas Hild, Dionys Ottl

Hild und K is an ambitious group of young architects led by Andreas Hild and Dionys Ottl. In addition to exhibiting at the Venice Biennale, Hild und K has realized several buildings in Germany ranging from small bus stops to town planning. Their well-known projects include a big paint warehouse in Eichstätt, the "Small Theatre" in Landshut, and a massive exhibition space in Munich.

www.hildundk.de

1 Exhibitionbuilding, *construction site 2004, Riem, Munich*
2 Allianz arena, *loge 2005*

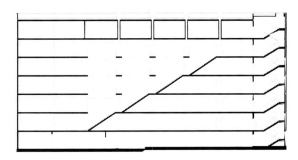

2

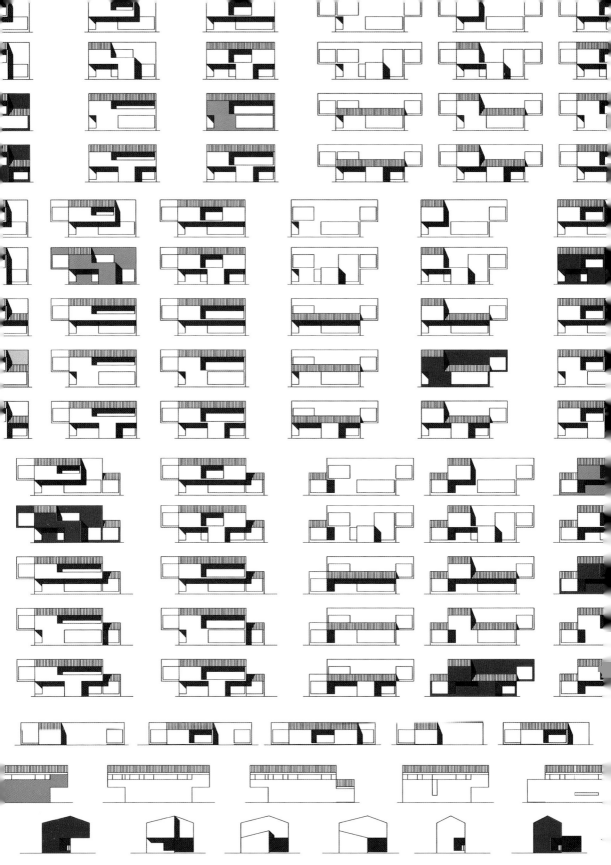

HUTTUNEN-LIPASTI-PAKKANEN | HELSINKI, FINLAND
Santeri Lipasti, Pekka Pakkanen, Risto Huttunen

Projects built throughout Europe demonstrate Huttunen-Lipasti-Pakkanen's capacity for great stylistic variety and formal complexity. Before beginning their own practice in 1997, the members of the firm gained experience through years of working for international architecture offices. The strength of their work is found in their attention to the building's context as well as their intuition for material detailing.

www.huttunen-lipasti.fi

1 prefabricated steelframe housing system 2005, *living design competition*
2 Atelier Laukamo 2003, *Espoo, Finland*

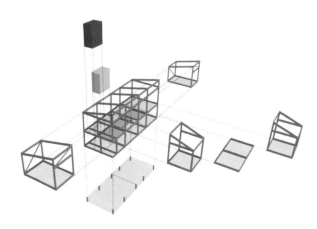

IAN+ | ROME, ITALY

Carmelo Baglivo, Luca Galofaro, Stefania Manna

IaN+ was founded in 1997 as a place where the theory and practice of architecture can overlap and intersect. Each project questions the contemporary urban condition through architecture and redefines the concept of territory as a relational space between the landscape and its human user. Architecture is thus conceived as a method endowed with independence, a programmatic and topological diagram that is perpetually updated.

www.ianplus.it

1 Laboratori università di Tor Vergata 2004
2 Tittot glass museum 2004, *Taipei, Taiwan – international competition*
3 The Daugava Embankement Riga

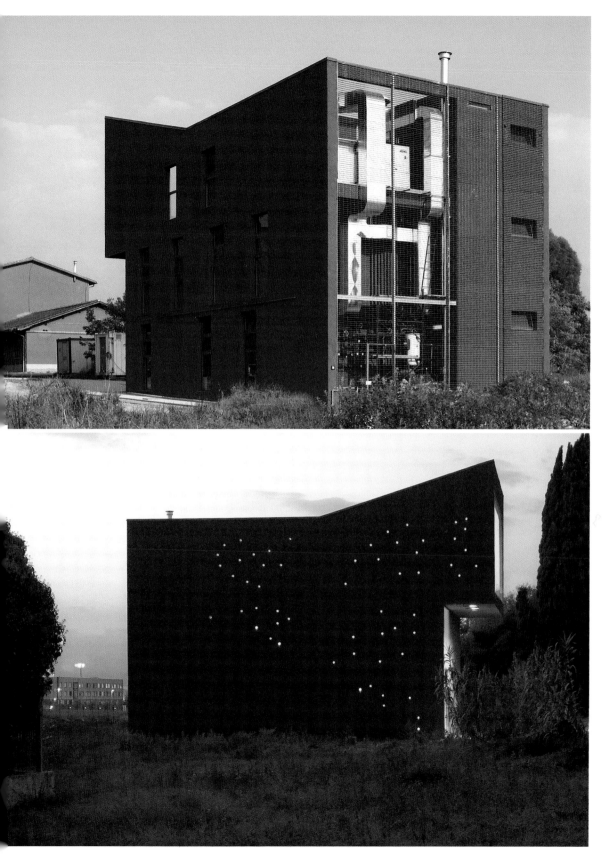

2

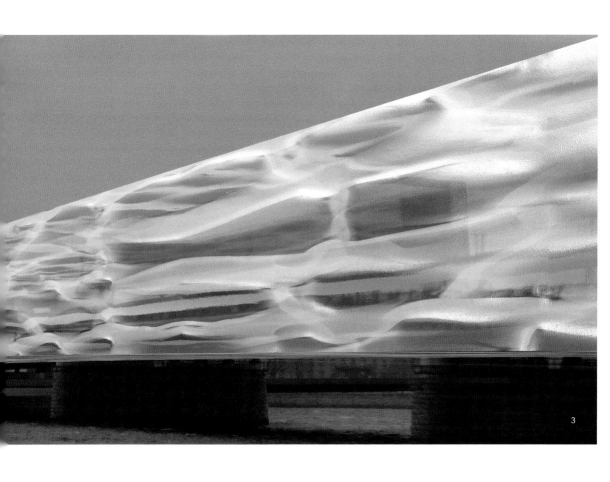

IPPOLITO FLEITZ GROUP | STUTTGART, GERMANY
Peter Ippolito, Gunter Fleitz

ippolito fleitz group is a multidisciplinary studio formed in 2002 by two Stuttgart architecture alumni. The studio focuses on giving their clients' complex identity an adequate form through a rigorous, creative approach to design. For ippolito fleitz group, identity is understood as a process whereby an idea is filtered through the lenses of architecture, communication, and design.

www.ifgroup.org

1 da Loretta Trattoria 2004, *Stuttgart*
2 Röwa, *trade fair exhibition system*
3 Sigrun Woehr, *shop design*

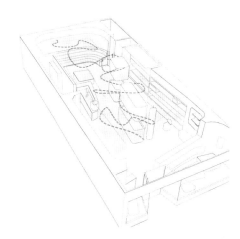

JOHANNES TORPE STUDIOS | COPENHAGEN, DENMARK
Johannes Torpe, Rune Reilly Kölsch

At 32, Johannes Torpe is already a designer with an international reputation for using his creativity and passion to communicate with others. His brother, DJ and producer Rune Reilly Kölsch, joined the company in 2001, enabling them to produce designs and music together and use their combined energy to build their brands: Johannes Torpe Studios, which concentrates on design, and Artificial Funk, which concentrates on music.

www.johannestorpe.com

1 Supergeil café 2001, *Copenhagen, Denmark*
2 NASA nightclub 2003, *Copenhagen, Denmark*

K ARCHITECTURES | PARIS, FRANCE
Karine Herman, Jérome Sigwalt

Established in 1993, k-architectures started their activities with international ideas competitions. To date, the office has completed four built projects – alone or in association with partners – such as an artist's workshop, an office building in Lille, and a gymnasium. Karine and Jérôme are also interested in design education; they both teach at different schools, accept invitations as lecturers, and direct university workshops.

www.k-architectures.com

Stu 2000, *Paris*

KCAP / ASTOC ARCHITECTS & PLANNERS |COLOGNE/ ROTTERDAM, GERMANY/THE NETHERLANDS

P. Berner, K. Christiaanse, R. Gietema, O. Hall, A. Kühn, M. Neppl, H. van den Born, I. van Oort

KCAP / ASTOC is working in a spectrum ranging from interior design to large-scale urban development. The office network is specialized in projects on the interface of architecture and urban design that deal with different scales and mixed programme use.

www.astoc.de

www.kcap.nl

1 Holzhafen Bürogebäude Ost 2003, *Hamburg*
2 DGAG / B&L Interior 2003, *Hamburg*
3 Kennedy Business Center 2003, *Eindhoven, Niederlande*
4 Herti 6 2005, *Zug, Schweiz*

1

3

4

4

KOSMOS | TALLINN, ESTONIA
Ott Kadarik, Villem Tomiste, Mihkel Tüür

Starting in 2002 with three members, Kosmos has since expanded to a team of seven people who together have been realizing projects in and around their home city of Tallinn in Estonia. Their architectural designs include multi-family housing, city planning projects, public space designs, and single-family residences.

www.kosmoses.ee

1 Center square of Rakvere
2 Group of apartment houses, *Saue Parish, Laagri*

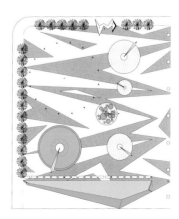

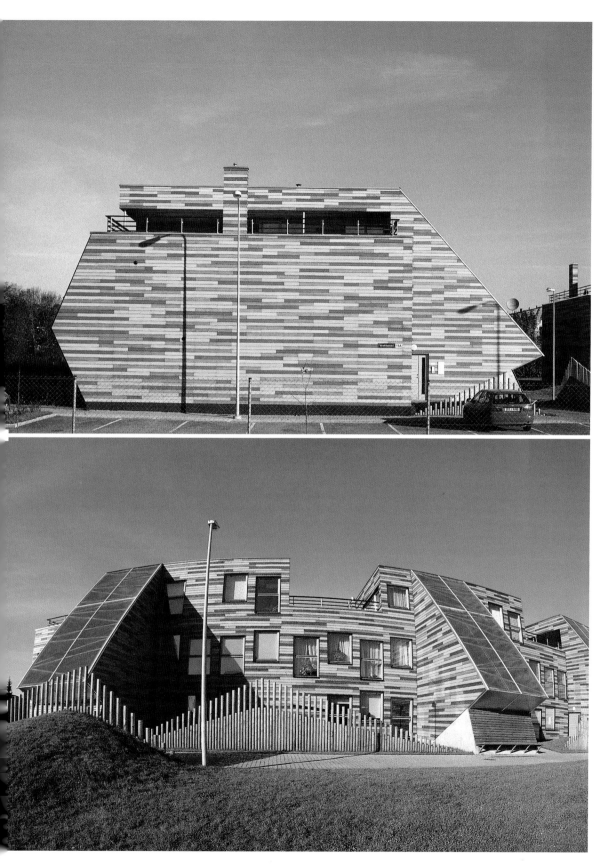

KUBA & PILAŘ ARCHITEKTI | BRNO, CZECH REPUBLIC
Ladislav Kuba, Tomáš Pilař

Kuba & Pilař architekti has existed since 1996 when the partners began to enter and participate in architectural competitions together. They obtained their first commissions through success in these competitions, and continue to follow that pattern today with innovative concepts for libraries, housing, and public buildings.

www.arch.cz/kuba.pilar

1 Faculty of Arts Library 2002, *Masaryk University in Brno*
2 Moravian-Silesian Research Library 2007, *Ostrava*
3 Housing Development Tichá Šárka 2006, *Prague*

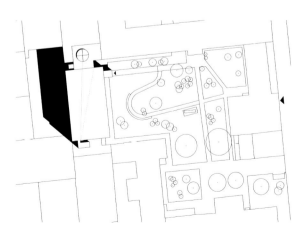

LENS ASS | HASSELT, BELGIUM
Bart Lens

Bart Lens started his own firm in 1996 after collecting inspiration and experience in other offices. He has won several different competitions and awards; his work has been featured in books, television, and magazines. His vision is to make the design process tangible through careful planning and synthesis of ideas at every scale.

www.lensass.be

1 Lowet Appeltans 2004, *private house*
2 Donum, lifestyle gallery, *2001 restoration, interior and renovation of the former post office to a design gallery with lofts*
3 LENS ASS 2002, *renovation of a commercial building to an architecture office with loft, Hasselt, Belgium*

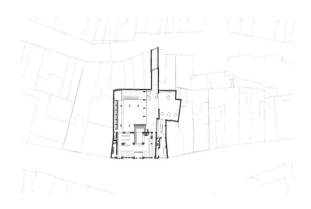

1

3

LETZEL FREIVOGEL | HALLE / SAALE, GERMANY
Nadja Letzel, Gábor Freivogel

Nadja Letzel and Gábor Freivogel studied architecture at the famous university at Weimar, where they received their diplomas. The cities of Kassel, Glasgow, and Cottbus were just intermediate stops for both architects before they moved to Halle an der Saale and started letzel freivogel in 1998. Since then they have won many first prizes in competitions, some of which – like the multimedia center in mid-Germany – have been realized.

www.letzelfreivogel.de

Multimedia center in mid-Germany 2006, *Halle / Saale*

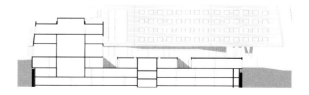

LIVERANI / MOLTENI | MILAN, ITALY

Enrico Molteni, Andrea Liverani

Liverani/Molteni architetti was founded in Milan in 1999. The partners see design as an intellectual and rational act to be accomplished at a variety of scales through research and careful consideration of programmatic needs. These aspirations have been demonstrated in their award-winning competition entries and built work.

www.liverani-molteni.it

1 St House 2003, *Barlassina, Milan*
2 New town hall 2004, *Seregno*

LÖHMANN'S ARCHITECTURE • URBAN + INDUSTRIAL DESIGN | AMSTERDAM, THE NETHERLANDS
Heike Löhmann

Löhmann's Architecture • Urban + Industrial Design was founded by Heike Löhmann in 1996. Their portfolio is characterized by uniqueness and variety; for Löhmann, the design process is not a fixed method, but an un-dogmatic approach developed specifically for each project and each individual client.

www.loehmann.nl

1 House Ouderkerk 2003, *Ouderkerk aan de Amstel*
2 House Rijkaart 2002, *Hoevelaken*

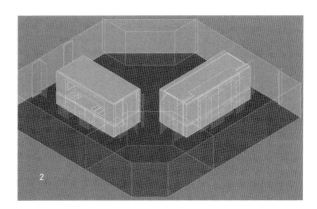

M41LH2 | **HELSINKI, FINLAND**
Johanna Hyrkäs, Tommi Mäkynen, Tuomas Siitonen

M41LH2 is a Helsinki-based architecture and design office formed in 2001 and comprised of artists, graphic designers, and architects. Although they began their practice with getting commissions to create bar and club interiors, they have lately extended into a larger scale to include architectural projects and urban design.

www.m41lh2.com

Helsinki Club 2003, *in association with Anteeksi*

MAECHTIG VRHUNC | LJUBLJANA, SLOVENIA
Tomaz Maechtig, Ursa Vrhunc

Maechtig Vrhunc Architekti is a small, progressive firm that prides itself on design intelligence and technical competence. Their approach integrates contemporary thinking and experimentation with professional, project-driven logic. Their architecture challenges traditional pre-conceptions of space and subverts the normative narrative with innovative, effective, and emotionally rich design.

www.mvarch.com

1 MVA office 2004, *Ljubljana, Slovenia*
2 Mostec Housing 2001
3 Campus Novo mesto 2005, *competition for a university campus for 3.500 students*

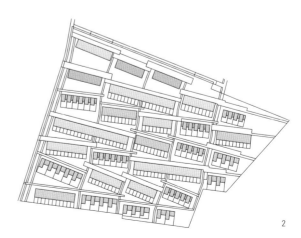

2

2

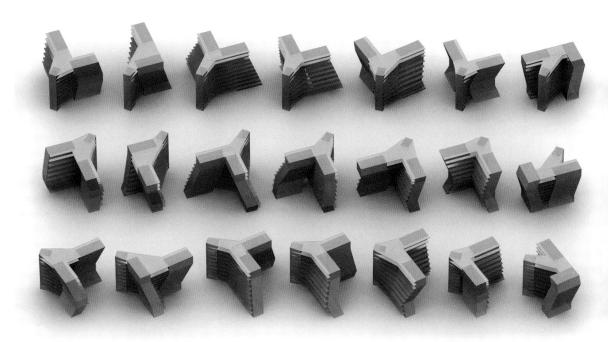

MAP | VENICE, ITALY
Francesco Magnani, Traudy Pelzel

Francesco Magnani and Traudy Pelzel started to work together in 2002. MaP deals with architecture and town planning projects in public and private commissions as well as
national and international architectural competitions. Since
2003 the office has been engaged in an intense partner-
ship with Nicola Busato's architectural office in Vicenza: a
pavilion for disabled people is now under construction near
Vicenza.

www.map-studio.it

1 "Il Tempio Vaticano Carlo Fontana 1694" 2004, *S.Maurizio
church in Venice*
2 Villabona 2003, *urban development plan for the
Villabona area, Venice*

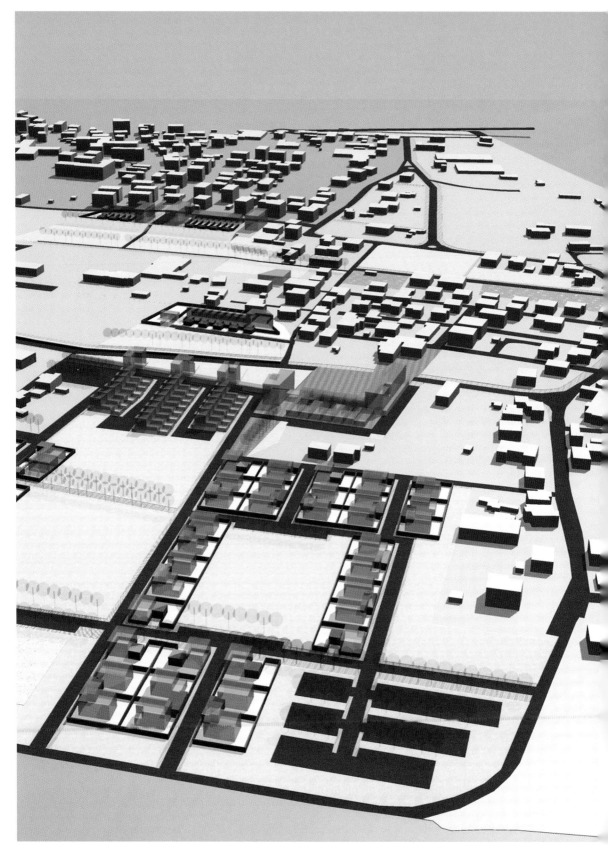

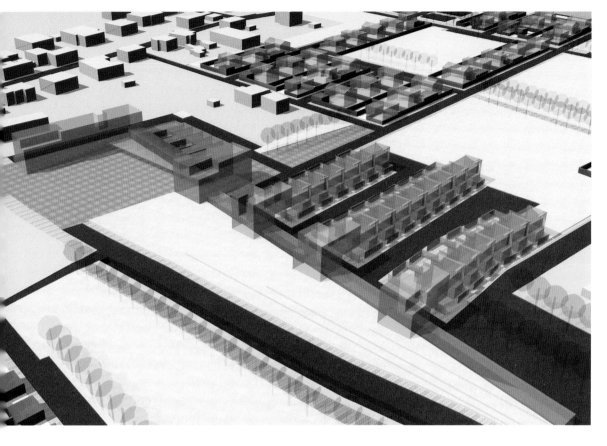

MARGE | STOCKHOLM, SWEDEN

Katarina Grundsell, Louise Masreliez, Pye Aurell Ehrström, Susanne Ramel

Marge Arkitekter, established in 2002, works on various projects at different scales such as housing, interior design, product design, and urban planning. To attach strong ideas to their projects, they combine critical analysis and concept development with an optimistic approach to design.

www.marge.se

1 Villa 1.0 2004, *prefabricated house, Stockholm, Sweden*
2 Alcro designers ad.05 2005, *Stockholm, Sweden*
3 Arcö 2005, *private house, Arkösund, Sweden*
4 Museum of Modern Art 2004, *interior design, Stockholm, Sweden*

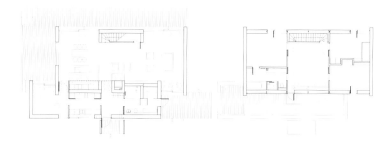

4

MINUSPLUS | BUDAPEST, HUNGARY
Zsolt Alexa, Donát Rabb, Ákos Schreck

Since 2002 this young Hungarian team has been devoted to experimental design methods, with the aim of integrating a wide range of media into their work. One of their challenges is to keep up with the latest information technologies, to be able to understand and use state-of-the-art digital tools. They also strive to create a truly interdisciplinary practice through cooperation with researchers from other fields.

www.minusplus.hu

1 János Arany Primary School and special school for mentally disabled 2004, *Csorna, Hungary, with Tamas Karácsony*
2 Atelier house 2005, *Reitter Ferenc utcai Műteremház, with Mihály Balázs*

MUF ARCHITECTURE/ART | LONDON, UK
Liza Fior, Katherine Clarke

Formed in 1994, muf architecture/art is a collaborative practice committed to public projects that embed enduring and unexpected interventions into the physical and social fabric of the urban environment. Their interdisciplinary practice has pioneered innovative methods of working directly with communities to deliver design-led projects that reveal and value the desires and experiences of varied constituencies.

www.muf.co.uk

The Hypocaust Building 2004, *St. Albans*

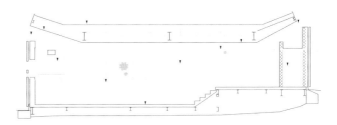

NO W HERE | STUTTGART, GERMANY
Henning Volpp, Karl Amann

no w here was founded in 1999 in Stuttgart by Karl Amann and Henning Volpp. Since 2003 they have also been collaborating with Sibylle Heeg in Gesellschaft für Soziales Planen mbH. Their latest built project – the Domsingschule in Stuttgart – is about to be completed. Each of their schemes, whether architecture, furniture, or interiors, is a carefully constructed answer to a specific design problem.

www.nowherearchitekten.de

1 Showroom Catalano, *Stuttgart*
2 Domsingschule 2006, *Stuttgart*

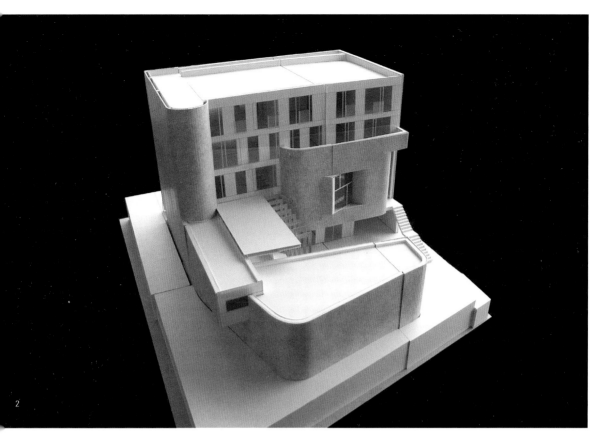

2

OFIS | LJUBLJANA, SLOVENIA
Rok Oman, Spela Videcnik

Ofis arhitekti, based in Ljubljana, Slovenia, was formed by Rok Oman and Spela Videcnik. Their work negotiates between urban proposals and architecture, between interior design and performing arts. Their numerous built projects have received several international awards and have been published worldwide.

www.ofis-a.si

1 Villa Bled "under" extension 2004, *extension of 19th-century villa*
2 Social housing blocks on the coast
3 Private mini loft 2002
4 The extension and renovation of the City Museum Ljubljana 2005

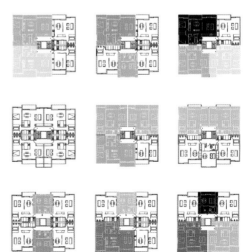

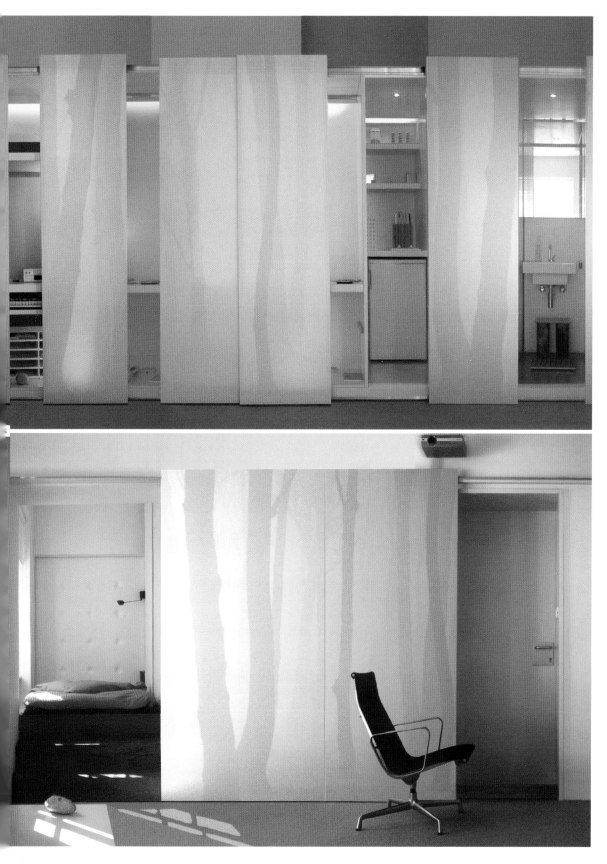

4

OGRIS.WANEK ARCHITECTS| KLAGENFURT, AUSTRIA

Gerfried Ogris, Ralf Wanek

Although ogris.wanek architects was established in 2003, the two partners had worked together previously on several other projects. They view architecture as a cultural and social value necessary for a working society. As a basic principle for their work, they see not only the relationships between space and observer, space and volume, space and emotion, space and expectation, but also space and presence and – not least – space and space.

www.ogriswanek.com

1 big 2005, *extension of a building of the 60s*
2 red, *inner organization and optimization of a dwelling*

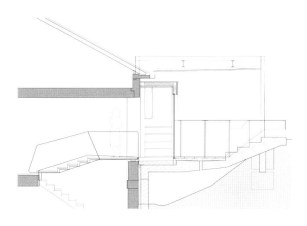

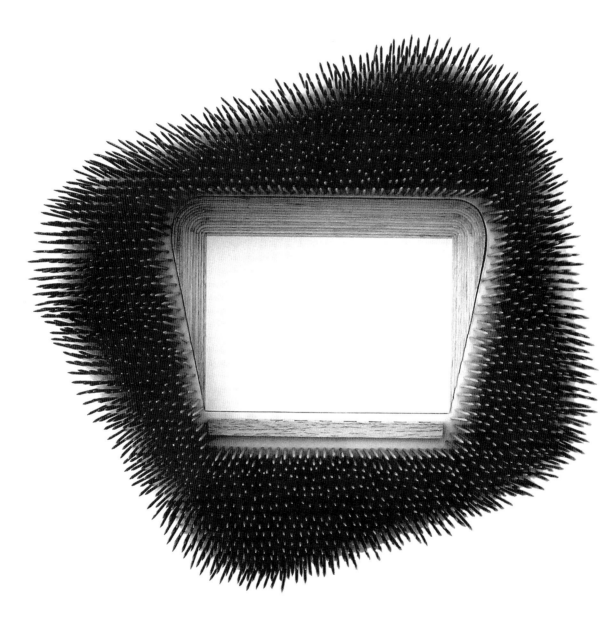

PLANO B | LISBON, PORTUGAL
Eduardo Carvalho, Francisco Freire, Luís Gama

"Plano B" is an alternative to the initial plan, an option to take when the unexpected occurs. Plano B Arquitectura takes this definition seriously when it comes to developing material solutions and building prototypes. Using wood, earth, or straw (as an option) along with steel or concrete (as a need) allows them to reflect upon the ethical, social, political, and economical aspects of ecology in an industrialized context.

www.planob.com

1 Soccer field 2004, *competition for Syiathemba, South Africa*
2 Work camp 2003, *Colares, Portugal*
3 Agricultural warehouses 2004, *Samouco, Portugal*

PLASMA | LONDON, UK
Holger Kehne, Eva Castro

Founded in 1999, Plasma Studio is an innovative architecture and design practice based in London and northern Italy. Partners Eva Castro and Holger Kehne combine academic research with the uncompromising implementation of high-quality residential, commercial, and leisure projects. Their pragmatism and radical thinking helped them win the prestigious Corus/Building Design Young Architect of the Year Award.

www.plasmastudio.com

1 Hotel Puerta America 2005, *rooms and common spaces for a new luxury hotel*
2 Minerva Street Loft 2003 , *live/work refurbishment*

1

PLOT = BJARKE INGELS GROUP (BIG) AND JULIEN'S DESIGN STUDIO (JDS) | COPENHAGEN, DENMARK

Julien De Smedt, Bjarke Ingels

PLOT was founded in Copenhagen in 2001 by architects Julien De Smedt and Bjarke Ingels in order to develop an architectural practice that turns intense research and analysis of practical and theoretical issues into the driving forces of design. In 2006, after five successful years, the two founders of Plot decided to go their separate ways. Julien founded Julien's Design Studio (JDS) and Bjarke founded Bjarke Ingels Group (BIG).

www.big.dk

www.jdsarchitects.dk

1 VM, dwellings in Orestad 2005, *220 housing units in Copenhagen*
2 Stavanger Concert Hall, *competition*
3 Maritime Youth House 2004, *cultural house*

2

3

3

PUNKTAS | VILNIUS, LITHUNIA

Martynas Nagelė, Marius Kanevičius, Augustas Audėjaitis,
Andrius Skiezgelas, Vytautas Biekša, Rokas Kilčiauskas

PUNKTAS is a group of six young Lithuanian architects working together in a workshop studio situation. The essential
objective of PUNKTAS is the progressive management of
the creative process that ultimately leads to an expressive,
responsible architecture. They have been employing this
mode of practice since 2001.

www.punktas.com

Moscow Center, *Vilnius, Lithunia*

SABARCHITEKTEN | BASEL, SWITZERLAND

Markus Kägi, Andreas Reuter, Dominique Salathé, Thomas Schnabel

The four architects of sabarchitekten joined forces in 1997 to develop their ideas and projects within their own firm. The sabarchitekten portfolio ranges from single-family homes to bigger developments and urban planning assignments. Spatial plasticity and a sensitive approach to materials are keys to anchoring sabarchitekten's designs in their environment as site-specific structures.

www.sabarchitekten.ch

1 One family house Wissler 2005, *Neuwiller, Alsace, France*
2 Reconstruction of an old mill 2005, *living and publishing house, office building, Stähle Mühle, Germany*
3 New schoolbuilding 2004, *integrated theatre, La Tour-de-Treme, Switzerland*

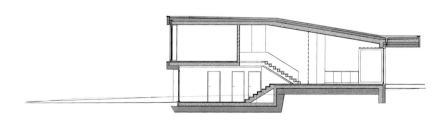

1

SHARE ARCHITECTS | VIENNA, AUSTRIA
Silvia Forlati, Hannes Bürger, Thomas Lettner

Share architects was founded in summer 2003 in Vienna by Silvia Forlati, Hannes Bürger and Thomas Lettner. The studio is based in an old metal workshop in Vienna's 8th district refurbished by the practice itself. As the name implies, they see design as a research based, collaborative process, where ideas, wishes, and dreams are shared and space is made for them in a creative, solution-oriented architecture.

www.share-arch.com

1 Creamflo, *Reshaping space for piano music and living, Vienna*
2 House Ö, *8m x 30m living under folded roofscape*

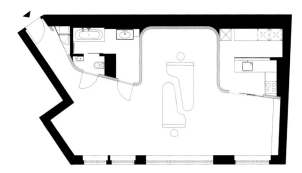

2

S.H.S ARCHITEKTI | PRAGUE, CZECH REPUBLIC
Lubor Sladký, Lukáš Holub

S.H.S architekti was founded by Lukáš Holub and Lubor Sladký in 1998. Their architecture studio offers design services for all kinds of projects, including cultural institutions, housing, industrial buildings, urban planning, engineering, interior design, and construction management.

www.shsarch.cz

1 Living house for young families 2001, *Třebóň, with M.Buřičová, L.Holub, L.Sladký*
2 Central fire station 2004, *airport Prague 6, with L.Sladký, co. L.Holub, T.Ajmová*
3 Modern gallery of the academy of fine arts 2004, *reconstruction and extension, Prague, with Z.Jiran (JKA), M.Kohout (JKA), L.Holub, V. Kvapilová*

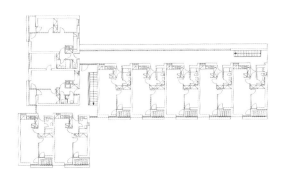

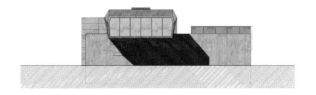

2

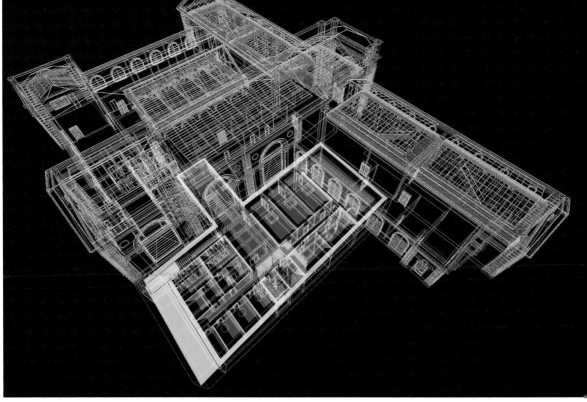

3

SPRINGETT MACKAY | LONDON, UK
Matthew Springett, Kirsteen Mackay

Since 2000, Springett Mackay has completed a number of private and commercial projects in the UK and Ireland. In 2006 the practice started work on its first built project in the Netherlands. Other Springett Mackay projects include an open-air market, an aviary and visitor's center, and landscaping for a school in London.

www.sm-arch.com

1 Pool
2 newhouse
3 conversion

2

3

STUDIJA LAPE | VILNIUS, LITHUNIA
Tomas Lape, Ruta Kijauskaite, Darius Mitka

studija lape was founded in 2004 in Vilnius, Lithuania by members Tomas Lape and Ruta Kijauskaite. They were later joined by Darius Mitka. Their clean, bold work embraces not only architecture but also interior design and cooperate identity.

www.lape.lt

1 Interior of living house 2005, *apartments in suburbs of Vilnius*
2 Living house for two families 2005, *house in suburbs of Vilnius*
3 Constructus 2005, *interior of multistory office building*
4 Gera Pramoga 2005, *interior of event organization company*

STUDIO NEX | BARCELONA, SPAIN
Ellen Rapelius, Xavier Franquesa

In 1995, a German architect and a Catalan designer drew from their years of experience at different European offices to build a solid background of professional practice for their studio in Barcelona. Studio Nex's work has been recognized with an FAD Prizes Selection and in numerous international publications.

www.stnex.com

1 Dormi Boutique, *Barcelona*
2 Lupino, restaurant and lounge, *Barcelona*
3 Dot light club, *Barcelona*

2

3

STUDIO PARETAIA | STUTTGART, GERMANY
Susanne Müller-Schöll, Axel Müller-Schöll

Prof. Axel Müller-Schöll and Susanne Müller-Schöll both studied in Stuttgart and Florence; they have been working together as a team since 1986 in their office in Stuttgart. Furniture and interior designs diversify Studio Paretaia's architectural portfolio. They have participated in several exhibitions at home and abroad.

www.paretaia.de

1 Headquarter Diakonie, Stuttgart 2005
2 Private guesthouse, Tengen 2004

2

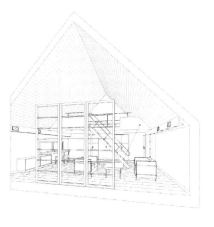

STUDIO X DESIGN GROUP | TREVISO, ITALY

Lara Rettondini, Oscar Brito

Studio X Design Group is a multidisciplinary practice founded in 2000 by Lara Rettondini and Oscar Brito and specializ-
ing in architecture, design, and communication. Their work
includes projects for fashion brands like the new concept
for the Mandarina Duck shops worldwide.

www.stxdesign.com

1 Mandaring, Mandarina Duck retail concept, *Paris flagship*
2 Circuit Box 2004, *minimal dwelling concept, Tokyo*

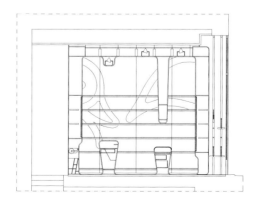

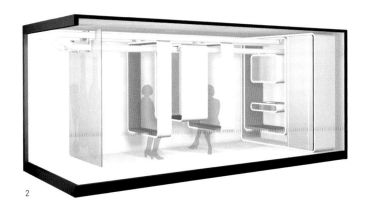

2

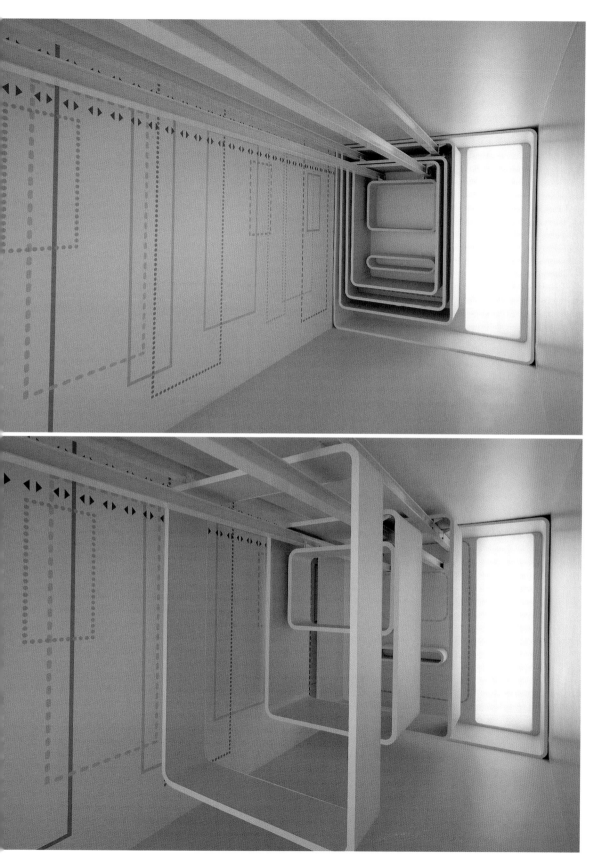

SURFACE | LONDON, UK
Richard Scott, Andy MacFee

Richard Scott studied at the Bartlett with Peter Cook, worked for Will Alsop, and taught at the Bartlett and the Architectural Association in London. Andy MacFee worked for Will Alsop and was project architect for Peckham Library. Their work has won several awards and has been exhibited at RIBA and at the Victoria and Albert Museum's "40 under 40" exhibition.

www.surfacearchitects.com

1 Queen Mary, Lock-keepers Graduate Centre 2005,
  contemporary extension of old cottage, Mile End, London
2 Ambiguous object

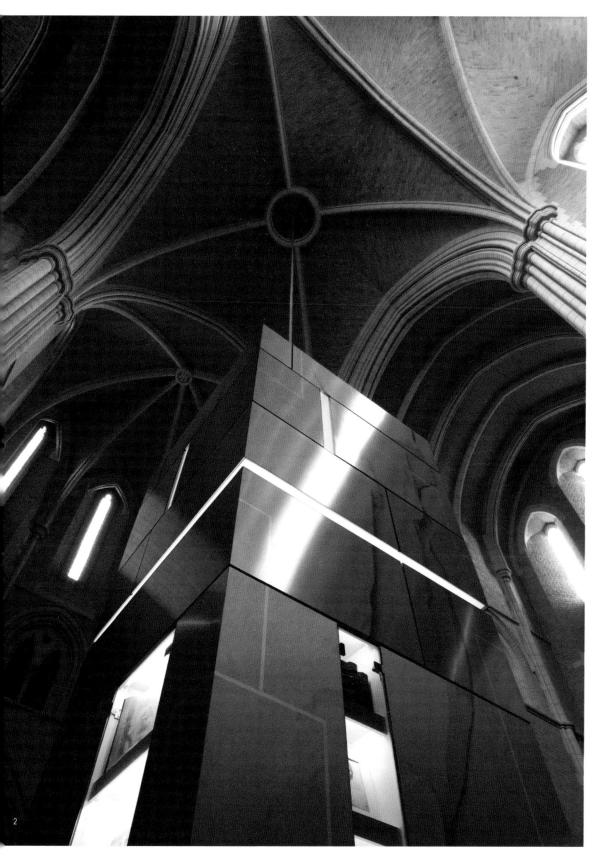

SVA | LJUBLJANA, SLOVENIA
Jurij Sadar, Bostjan Vuga

In less than ten years, Sadar Vuga Architects has positioned itself as one of the critical European architectural practices. Since its beginning, SVA has won seven competitions and designed about 100 projects – twenty of which have been implemented. SVA does not specialize in a particular branch of architectural design; with its inventive, challenging approach, it covers a wide production spectrum, from urban planning to interior design.

www.sadarvuga.com

1 Condominium Trnovski Pristan in Ljubljana 2004, *residential building*
2 Apartment house Gradaska 2003, *residential building, Ljubljana*
3 Panoramic garden of chamber of commerce and industry of Slovenia CCIS office building 2003, *covered attic, Ljubljana*

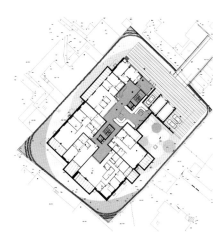

Ü.NN | ATTENDORN, GERMANY
Oliver Rüsche, Tobias Willers

ü.NN was founded in 2004 in Attendorn by Oliver Rüsche and Tobias Willers, two years after they collaborated on an exhibition project called "zimmer_frei." In their quest for flexible, communicative structures, ü.NN is interested in every aspect of the design of space. Ten of their projects have been realized so far.

www.uenn.de

1 House Hahn 2005, *Attendorn, Germany*
2 House Segref 2004, *Finnentrop*

2

2

URBAN OFFICE ARCHITECTURE | MILAN, ITALY

Carlo Frugiuele, Massimo Marinelli

Urban Office Architecture is an award-winning architectural design firm established in 1998 with offices in both New York City and Milan. Founders Carlo Frugiuele and Massimo Marinelli focus on design excellence and sustainability in an effort to suggest potential beyond the limitations of site, budget, and style. UOA's solutions are based on cutting-edge technologies and the visionary belief that architecture is an analogical and inspirational process.

www.uoa-architecture.com

1 OCF Artist shelter 2002, *residential, working space, Milan, Italy*
2 Ikea store 1999, *Milan, Italy*
3 Gramercy Park Residence 2004, *New York City*

3

WEBER + WÜRSCHINGER | BERLIN, GERMANY
Michael Weber, Klaus Würschinger

Weber+Würschinger is dedicated to the design and realization of architectural concepts in collaboration with partners such as urban designers, landscape architects, and
engineers. The central concern is a smooth interaction of
layout, design, and material. Their dialogue with the client
is a guiding principle and defines all qualifications for a
project.

www.weberwuerschinger.com

1. Extension/increase of an office building 2001,
   Weiden, Bavaria
2. Metamophosis of a storehouse 2005, *Weiden, Bavaria*
3. Skin of storagehall "Gelöcherte Fassade" 2002,
   Weiden, Bavaria
4. New office structure 2004, *Rehau, Bavaria*

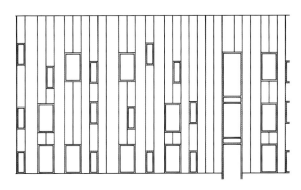

3

ZD6 | PORTO MAGHERA, ITALY
Paolo Ceccon, Marco Ferretto, Francesco Magro

zD6 was established in 2002 by Paolo Ceccon, Marco Ferretto, and Francesco Magro. The office designs interiors,
public spaces, transportation infrastructure, buildings, and
urban environments. They started a collaborating with Ric-
cardo Palmieri from the beginning on.

www.zD6.it

1 Bortolozzo house, *interior design of a private house*
2 Laguna medical center, *interior design*
3 G house, *interior design*

3

ZIZI & YOYO | TALLINN, ESTONIA
Yoko Alender, Veronika Valk

Zizi & YoYo is a freshly established architecture and urban event-making office located in Tallinn, Estonia. Partners Yoko Alender and Veronika Valk deal with human habitats on all levels, aiming at radical, experiential, and experimental urban events. Their constructed works include public and private buildings, interiors, and landscape design.

1 Composer Tubin's Memorial, *Tartu*
2 Suure-Jaani Sports Centre

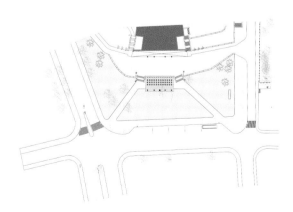

INDEX

© 2006 daab
cologne london new york

published and distributed worldwide by
daab gmbh
friesenstr. 50
d - 50670 köln

p +49 - 221 - 913 927 0
f +49 - 221 - 913 927 20

mail@daab-online.com
www.daab-online.com

publisher ralf daab
rdaab@daab-online.com

creative director feyyaz
mail@feyyaz.com

editorial project by fusion publishing gmbh stuttgart . los angeles
© 2006 fusion publishing, www.fusion-publishing.com

editor katharina feuer

layout kerstin graf, papierform
imaging jan hausberg

photo credits
coverphoto front plot=big and jds
coverphoto back die photodesigner
introduction page 7 fuhrimann / hächler, 9 die photodesigner, 11 killian o'sullivan
imprint page 399 nicola belluzzi
text introduction katharina feuer
translations by ade team übersetzungen / stuttgart, claudia ade
english translation dr. andrea adelung
french translation jocelyne abarca
spanish translation sara costa-sengera
italian translation jacqueline rizzo

printed in slovenia
mkt print d.d., slovenia
www.mkt-print.com

isbn-10   3-937718-72-9
isbn-13   978-3-937718-72-9